2017 Weekly Planner

To My Daughter, I Love You

Susan Polis Schutz

Illustrated by Stephen Schutz

GW00602806

Blue Mountain Arts®
Boulder, Colorado

Monday, December 26, 2016

Tuesday, December 27, 2016

Wednesday, December 28, 2016

Thursday, December 29, 2016

Friday, December 30, 2016

Saturday, December 31, 2016

Sunday, January 1, 2017

You are a shining
example of what a
daughter can be —
loving and compassionate
beautiful and good
honest and principled
determined and independent
sensitive and intelligent
You are a shining
example of what every
mother wishes her
daughter were
and I
am so very
proud of
you

January 2017

Sunday	Monday	Tuesday	Wednesday
1 New Year's Day	2 Bank Holiday (UK)	3 Bank Holiday (Scotland)	4
8	9	10	11
15	16 Martin Luther King, Jr.'s Birthday Observed (USA)	17	18
22	23	24	25
29	30	31	

Notes:

Thursday	Friday	Saturday
5	6	7
	Epiphany	
12	13	14
Full Moon ○		
19	20	21
26	27	28
Australia Day (Australia)		Chinese New Year

December 2016

S	M	T	W	T	F	S
				1	2	3
4	5	6	7	8	9	10
11	12	13	14	15	16	17
18	19	20	21	22	23	24
25	26	27	28	29	30	31

February

S	M	T	W	T	F	S
			1	2	3	4
5	6	7	8	9	10	11
12	13	14	15	16	17	18
19	20	21	22	23	24	25
26	27	28				

Monday, January 2
Bank Holiday (UK)

Tuesday, January 3
Bank Holiday (Scotland)

Wednesday, January 4

Thursday, January 5

Friday, January 6
Epiphany

Saturday, January 7

Sunday, January 8

To My Daughter with Love on the Important Things in Life

A mother tries to provide her daughter
   with insight
into the important things in life
in order to make her life
as happy and fulfilling as possible

A mother tries to teach her daughter
to be good, always helpful to other people
to be fair, treating others equally
to have a positive attitude
to make things right when they are wrong
to know herself well
to know what her talents are
to set goals for herself
to not be afraid of working too hard to reach
   her goals...

(continued)

Monday, January 9

Tuesday, January 10

Wednesday, January 11

Thursday, January 12   Full Moon ○

Friday, January 13

Saturday, January 14

Sunday, January 15

A mother tries to teach her daughter
to have many interests to pursue
to laugh and have fun every day
to appreciate the beauty of nature
to enter into friendships with good people
to honor their friendships and always be
   a true friend
to appreciate the importance of the family
and to particularly respect and love our
   elder members
to use her intelligence at all times
to listen to her emotions
to adhere to her values...

(continued)

Monday, January 16   Martin Luther King, Jr.'s Birthday Observed (USA)

Tuesday, January 17

Wednesday, January 18

Thursday, January 19

Friday, January 20

Saturday, January 21

Sunday, January 22

A mother tries to teach her daughter
to not be afraid to stick to her beliefs
to not follow the majority when the majority is wrong
to realize that she is a woman equal to all men
to carefully plan a life for herself
to vigorously follow her chosen path
to enter into a relationship with someone worthy of herself
to love this person unconditionally with her body and mind
to share all that she has learned in life with this person

If I have provided you with an insight
into most of these things
then I have succeeded as a mother
in what I hoped to accomplish in raising you
If some of these things slipped by
while we were all so busy
I have a feeling that you know them anyway
And I certainly hope that you always continue to know
how much love and admiration
I have for you
my beautiful daughter

Monday, January 23

Tuesday, January 24

Wednesday, January 25

Thursday, January 26   Australia Day (Australia)

Friday, January 27

Saturday, January 28   Chinese New Year

Sunday, January 29

$\mathcal{M}$y day becomes wonderful
when I see your
pretty face smiling so sweetly
There is such warmth and intelligence
radiating from you
It seems that every day
you grow smarter and more beautiful
and every day
I am more proud of you...

(continued)

Monday, January 30

Tuesday, January 31

Wednesday, February 1   Black History Month Begins

Thursday, February 2   Groundhog Day

Friday, February 3

Saturday, February 4

Sunday, February 5

As you go through different stages of life
you should be aware that there will be many times
when you will feel scared and confused
but with your strength and values
you will always end up wiser
and you will have grown from your experiences
understanding more about people and life
I have already gone through
these stages
So if you need advice or someone to talk to
to make sense out of it all
I hope that you will talk to me
as I am continually cheering for your happiness
my sweet daughter
and I love you

February 2017

Sunday	Monday	Tuesday	Wednesday
			1 Black History Month Begins
5	**6** Waitangi Day (New Zealand)	**7**	**8**
12 Lincoln's Birthday (USA)	**13**	**14** Valentine's Day	**15**
19	**20** Presidents' Day (USA)	**21**	**22** Washington's Birthday (USA)
26	**27**	**28**	

Thursday	Friday	Saturday
2	3	4
Groundhog Day		
9	10	11
	Full Moon ◯	
16	17	18
23	24	25

January

S	M	T	W	T	F	S
1	2	3	4	5	6	7
8	9	10	11	12	13	14
15	16	17	18	19	20	21
22	23	24	25	26	27	28
29	30	31				

March

S	M	T	W	T	F	S
			1	2	3	4
5	6	7	8	9	10	11
12	13	14	15	16	17	18
19	20	21	22	23	24	25
26	27	28	29	30	31	

Notes:

Monday, February 6

Tuesday, February 7

Wednesday, February 8

Thursday, February 9

Friday, February 10 Full Moon ◯

Saturday, February 11

Sunday, February 12 Lincoln's Birthday (USA)

I looked at you today
and saw the same beautiful eyes
that looked at me with love
when you were a baby
I looked at you today
and saw the same beautiful mouth
that made me cry when you first smiled at me
when you were a baby
It was not long ago
that I held you in my arms
long after you fell asleep
and I just kept rocking you
all night long
I looked at you today
and saw my beautiful daughter
no longer a baby
but a beautiful person
with a full range of emotions, feelings
ideas and goals...

(continued)

Monday, February 13

Tuesday, February 14   Valentine's Day

Wednesday, February 15

Thursday, February 16

Friday, February 17

Saturday, February 18

Sunday, February 19

Every day is exciting
as I continue to watch you grow
I want you to always know that
in good and in bad times
I will love you
and that no matter what you do
or how you think
or what you say
you can depend on
my support, guidance
friendship and love
every minute of every day
I love being your mother

Monday, February 20 Presidents' Day (USA)

Tuesday, February 21

Wednesday, February 22 Washington's Birthday (USA)

Thursday, February 23

Friday, February 24

Saturday, February 25

Sunday, February 26

$\mathcal{I}$ know that lately you
have been having problems
and I just want you to know
that you can rely on me
for anything
you might need
But more important
keep in mind
that you are very capable
of dealing with any complications
that life has to offer
So
do whatever you must
feel whatever you must
and realize
that we all
grow wiser and
become more sensitive and
are able to enjoy life more
after we go through
hard times

Monday, February 27

Tuesday, February 28

Wednesday, March 1

Ash Wednesday
National Women's History Month Begins (USA)
St. David's Day (Wales)

Thursday, March 2

Friday, March 3

Saturday, March 4

Sunday, March 5

$\mathcal{A}$ woman will get only what she seeks
Choose your goals carefully
Know what you like
and what you do not like
Be critical about what you can do well
and what you cannot do well
Choose a career or lifestyle that interests you
and work hard to make it a success
but also have fun in what you do
Be honest with people
    and help them if you can
but don't depend on anyone
    to make life easy or happy for you
Only you can do that for yourself...

(continued)

March 2017

Sunday	Monday	Tuesday	Wednesday

February
S M T W T F S
    1 2 3 4
5 6 7 8 9 10 11
12 13 14 15 16 17 18
19 20 21 22 23 24 25
26 27 28
	April
	S M T W T F S
	          1
	2 3 4 5 6 7 8
	9 10 11 12 13 14 15
	16 17 18 19 20 21 22
	23/30 24 25 26 27 28 29
			1
			
			Ash Wednesday
			National Women's History
			Month Begins (USA)
			St. David's Day (Wales)

5	**6**	**7**	**8** International Women's Day
12 Purim Girl Scout Week Begins (USA) USA/Canada Daylight Saving Time Begins Full Moon ○	**13** Commonwealth Day (UK)	**14**	**15**
19	**20** Spring Begins	**21**	**22**
26 Mothering Sunday (UK) UK/Ireland Daylight Saving Time Begins	**27**	**28**	**29**

Notes:

Thursday	Friday	Saturday
2	3	4
9	10	11
16	17 St. Patrick's Day	18
23	24	25
30	31	

Monday, March 6

Tuesday, March 7

Wednesday, March 8   International Women's Day

Thursday, March 9

Friday, March 10

Saturday, March 11

Sunday, March 12   Purim
                                                    Girl Scout Week Begins (USA)
                                            USA/Canada Daylight Saving Time Begins
                                                                     Full Moon ○

$\mathcal{B}$e strong and decisive
but remain sensitive
Regard your family, and the idea of family
as the basis for security, support and love
Understand who you are
and what you want in life
before sharing your life with someone
When you are ready to enter a relationship
make sure that the person is worthy of
everything you are physically and mentally
Strive to achieve all that you want
Find happiness in everything you do
Love with your entire being
Love with an uninhibited soul
Make a triumph
of every aspect
of your life

A daughter is ✳ a rainbow bubble ✳ a star glimmering in the sky ✳ a rosebud after a storm ✳ a caterpillar turning into a butterfly

Monday, March 13

Commonwealth Day (UK)

Tuesday, March 14

Wednesday, March 15

Thursday, March 16

Friday, March 17

St. Patrick's Day

Saturday, March 18

Sunday, March 19

Notes:

Monday, March 20   Spring Begins

Tuesday, March 21

Wednesday, March 22

Thursday, March 23

Friday, March 24

Saturday, March 25

Sunday, March 26   Mothering Sunday (UK)
                                   UK/Ireland Daylight Saving Time Begins

You are so
precious to me
I love everything about you
If you are having a problem
I wish I were the one
having it and
I also wish I could
help you
If you are confused about
something difficult
just try to think about it
without barriers

My love for you
includes all difficulties
you will ever have
So remember
I am supporting you
and loving you
always

Monday, March 27

Tuesday, March 28

Wednesday, March 29

Thursday, March 30

Friday, March 31

Saturday, April 1   April Fools' Day

Sunday, April 2

$\mathcal{S}$ome people will be your friend
because of whom you know
Some people will be your friend
because of your position
Some people will be your friend
because of the way you look
Some people will be your friend
because of your possessions
But the only real friends
are the people who will be your friends
because they like you for how you are inside

April 2017

Sunday	Monday	Tuesday	Wednesday
	March S M T W T F S 1 2 3 4 5 6 7 8 9 10 11 12 13 14 15 16 17 18 19 20 21 22 23 24 25 26 27 28 29 30 31	May S M T W T F S 1 2 3 4 5 6 7 8 9 10 11 12 13 14 15 16 17 18 19 20 21 22 23 24 25 26 27 28 29 30 31	
2	**3**	**4**	**5**
9 Palm Sunday	**10**	**11** First Day of Passover Full Moon ○	**12**
16 Easter Sunday Orthodox Easter Sunday	**17** Easter Monday (Canada/ UK/Ireland/Australia)	**18**	**19**
23 St. George's Day (UK) **30**	**24** Holocaust Remembrance Day (Yom Hashoah)	**25** Anzac Day (Australia/New Zealand)	**26** Administrative Professionals Day

Notes:

Thursday	Friday	Saturday
		1
Try to choose your friends carefully. Make sure that they are worthy of you.		April Fools' Day
6	**7**	**8**
13	**14**	**15**
	Good Friday	
20	**21**	**22**
		Earth Day
27	**28**	**29**
Take Our Daughters and Sons to Work Day (USA)		

Monday, April 3

Tuesday, April 4

Wednesday, April 5

Thursday, April 6

Friday, April 7

Saturday, April 8

Sunday, April 9   Palm Sunday

*L*ean against a tree
and dream your world of dreams
Work hard at what you like to do
and try to overcome all obstacles
Laugh at your mistakes
and praise yourself for learning from them
Pick some flowers
and appreciate the beauty of nature
Be honest with people
and enjoy the good in them
Don't be afraid to show your emotions
Laughing and crying make you feel better
Love your friends and family with your entire being
They are the most important part of your life
Feel the calmness on a quiet sunny day
and plan what you want to accomplish in life
Find a rainbow
and live your
world of dreams

Monday, April 10

Tuesday, April 11

First Day of Passover
Full Moon ○

Wednesday, April 12

Thursday, April 13

Friday, April 14

Good Friday

Saturday, April 15

Sunday, April 16

Easter Sunday
Orthodox Easter Sunday

$\mathcal{W}$e cannot
listen to what
others want us
to do
We must listen
to ourselves
We don't need to
copy other people's ways
and we don't need to
act out certain lifestyles
to impress other people
Only we know
and only we can do what
is right for us...

(continued)

Monday, April 17

Easter Monday (Canada/UK/Ireland/Australia)

Tuesday, April 18

Wednesday, April 19

Thursday, April 20

Friday, April 21

Saturday, April 22

Earth Day

Sunday, April 23

St. George's Day (UK)

Start right now
You will need to
work very hard
You will need to
overcome many obstacles
You will need to go
against the better
judgment of many people
and you will need to
bypass their prejudices
But you can have
whatever you want
if you try hard enough
Start right now so that
you can live a life
designed by you and
for you —
a life you deserve

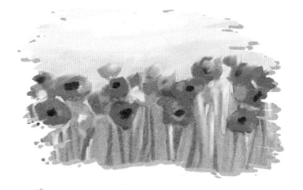

A daughter is ✳ hair flying in the wind ✳ red cheeks that glisten in the sunshine ✳ big daydream eyes

---

Monday, April 24   Holocaust Remembrance Day (Yom Hashoah)

Tuesday, April 25   Anzac Day (Australia/New Zealand)

Wednesday, April 26   Administrative Professionals Day

Thursday, April 27   Take Our Daughters and Sons to Work Day (USA)

Friday, April 28

Saturday, April 29

Sunday, April 30

Notes:

May 2017

Sunday	Monday	Tuesday	Wednesday
	1 May Day Bank Holiday (UK/Ireland)	2	3
7	8	9 National Teacher Day (USA)	10 Full Moon ○
14 Mother's Day	15	16	17
21	22 Victoria Day (Canada)	23	24
28	29 Memorial Day Observed (USA) Bank Holiday (UK)	30	31 First Day of Shavuot

Notes:

Thursday	Friday	Saturday
4	5	6
	Cinco de Mayo	
11	12	13
18	19	20
		Armed Forces Day (USA)
25	26	27
		First Day of Ramadan

April

S	M	T	W	T	F	S
						1
2	3	4	5	6	7	8
9	10	11	12	13	14	15
16	17	18	19	20	21	22
23/30	24	25	26	27	28	29

June

S	M	T	W	T	F	S
				1	2	3
4	5	6	7	8	9	10
11	12	13	14	15	16	17
18	19	20	21	22	23	24
25	26	27	28	29	30	

Monday, May 1

May Day
Bank Holiday (UK/Ireland)

Tuesday, May 2

Wednesday, May 3

Thursday, May 4

Friday, May 5

Cinco de Mayo

Saturday, May 6

Sunday, May 7

My little daughter
(but no longer little)
As you grow into a young adult —
a bouquet of beautiful, vigorous flowers
and I look at you with awe

Drink enough water of life
so you passionately blossom
When it is dark and cloudy
know that light will soon
shine through a clear sky

Absorb enough sunshine
to keep you warm
Absorb enough wind to flood you
with free-flowing movements

My young adult daughter
(but no longer little)
The fragrance of your world
will guide you
And I look at you with love

Monday, May 8

Tuesday, May 9   National Teacher Day (USA)

Wednesday, May 10   Full Moon ○

Thursday, May 11

Friday, May 12

Saturday, May 13

Sunday, May 14   Mother's Day

I Am *Always* Here for *You*

*S*ince you were born
you have been
such a beautiful
addition to our family
Now that you are growing up
I can see that
you are a beautiful
addition to the world
As I watch you
doing things on your own
I know you will find
happiness and success
because I am confident in
your ability
your self-knowledge
your values
But if you ever need a boost
or just someone to talk to
about difficulties
that might be occurring
I am always here
to help you
to understand you
to support you
and to love you

Monday, May 15

Tuesday, May 16

Wednesday, May 17

Thursday, May 18

Friday, May 19

Saturday, May 20   Armed Forces Day (USA)

Sunday, May 21

Sometimes I talk to you
and I am not really sure
what you are thinking
It is so important
to let your feelings
be known
Talk to someone
Write your feelings down
Create something based on your feelings
but do not keep them inside
Never be afraid to
be honest with people
and certainly never be afraid to
be honest with yourself
You are such an
interesting, sensitive, intelligent person
who has so much to share...

(continued)

Monday, May 22
Victoria Day (Canada)

Tuesday, May 23

Wednesday, May 24

Thursday, May 25

Friday, May 26

Saturday, May 27
First Day of Ramadan

Sunday, May 28

I want you to know
that wherever you go
or whatever you do
or whatever you think
you can always depend
on me, your mother
for complete and absolute
understanding
support
and love
forever

Monday, May 29

Tuesday, May 30

Wednesday, May 31

First Day of Shavuot

Thursday, June 1

Friday, June 2

Saturday, June 3

Sunday, June 4

Pentecost

*M*y daughter
when you were born
I held you in my arms
and just kept smiling at you
You always smiled back
your big eyes wide open
full of love
Now
as I watch you grow up
and become your own person
I look at you
your laughter
your happiness
your simplicity
your beauty
and I wonder where you will be
in fifteen years
and I wonder
where the world will be
in fifteen years
I just hope that you will
be able to enjoy a life
of sensitivity
goodness
accomplishment
and love
in a world that is at peace
But most of all
I want you to know that
I am very proud of you
and that I love you dearly

June 2017

Sunday	Monday	Tuesday	Wednesday

May						
S	M	T	W	T	F	S
	1	2	3	4	5	6
7	8	9	10	11	12	13
14	15	16	17	18	19	20
21	22	23	24	25	26	27
28	29	30	31			

July						
S	M	T	W	T	F	S
						1
2	3	4	5	6	7	8
9	10	11	12	13	14	15
16	17	18	19	20	21	22
23/30 24/31	25	26	27	28	29	

Sunday	Monday	Tuesday	Wednesday
4 Pentecost	5 Bank Holiday (Ireland)	6	7
11	12	13	14 Flag Day (USA)
18 Father's Day	19	20	21 Summer Begins
25 Eid al-Fitr	26	27	28

Thursday	Friday	Saturday
1	2	3
8	9 Full Moon ◯	10
15	16	17
22	23	24 St. Jean Baptiste Day (Québec)
29	30	

Notes:

Find happiness in everything you do.

Monday, June 5

Bank Holiday (Ireland)

Tuesday, June 6

Wednesday, June 7

Thursday, June 8

Friday, June 9

Full Moon ○

Saturday, June 10

Sunday, June 11

Notes:

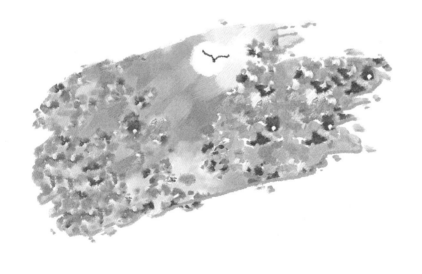

Monday, June 12

Tuesday, June 13

Wednesday, June 14 Flag Day (USA)

Thursday, June 15

Friday, June 16

Saturday, June 17

Sunday, June 18 Father's Day

So many times
you ask me questions
and your big beautiful eyes
look at me
with trust, confusion and
innocence
I hope that my
answers to you
will help guide you
Even though I always want to protect you
and step in for you when you have a
    difficult decision to make
it is very important that I do not interfere
so that you will learn from your
    own experiences
and develop confidence in your
    own judgment...

(continued)

Monday, June 19

Tuesday, June 20

Wednesday, June 21   Summer Begins

Thursday, June 22

Friday, June 23

Saturday, June 24   St. Jean Baptiste Day (Québec)

Sunday, June 25   Eid al-Fitr

There is a fine line between
a mother telling her daughter
too much
or too little
I hope I have struck a proper balance
I have always wanted to tell you
how honored I am that you
seek out my opinions
I appreciate the trust you have in me and
I want you to know that
I have an immense trust in you
I am very proud of you and
I love you

Monday, June 26

Tuesday, June 27

Wednesday, June 28

Thursday, June 29

Friday, June 30

Saturday, July 1   Canada Day (Canada)

Sunday, July 2

Daughter...

When you need someone
to talk to
I hope you will
talk to me

When you need someone
to laugh with
I hope you will
laugh with me

When you need someone
to advise you
I hope you will
turn to me

When you need someone
to help you
I hope you will
let me help you

I cherish and love
everything about you —
my beautiful daughter
And I will always support you
as a mother, as a person
and as a friend

July 2017

Sunday	Monday	Tuesday	Wednesday

June	August
S M T W T F S	S M T W T F S
1 2 3	1 2 3 4 5
4 5 6 7 8 9 10	6 7 8 9 10 11 12
11 12 13 14 15 16 17	13 14 15 16 17 18 19
18 19 20 21 22 23 24	20 21 22 23 24 25 26
25 26 27 28 29 30	27 28 29 30 31

2	3	4	5
		Independence Day (USA)	

9	10	11	12
Full Moon ◯			Bank Holiday (Northern Ireland)

16	17	18	19

23	24	25	26
30	31		

Thursday	Friday	Saturday
		1
	Only you can choose the lifestyle you want to follow.	Canada Day (Canada)
6	7	8
13	14	15
20	21	22
27	28	29

Notes:

Monday, July 3

Tuesday, July 4   Independence Day (USA)

Wednesday, July 5

Thursday, July 6

Friday, July 7

Saturday, July 8

Sunday, July 9   Full Moon ◯

$\mathcal{I}$ love the
respect and friendship that
we have discovered
with each other
It is so much fun
talking and going places
with you
We have a lot in common —
often seeing things
no one else notices
smelling things
no one else smells
observing and understanding people's obscure
peculiarities and characteristics
I enjoy being with you, Princess
and I love you

Monday, July 10

Tuesday, July 11

Wednesday, July 12   Bank Holiday (Northern Ireland)

Thursday, July 13

Friday, July 14

Saturday, July 15

Sunday, July 16

Monday, July 17

Tuesday, July 18

Wednesday, July 19

Thursday, July 20

Friday, July 21

Saturday, July 22

Sunday, July 23

Monday, July 24

Tuesday, July 25

Wednesday, July 26

Thursday, July 27

Friday, July 28

Saturday, July 29

Sunday, July 30

Sometimes I see you
confused
Sometimes I see you
troubled
Sometimes I see you
hurt
and I feel so sad and
helpless
I wish that I could absorb
these feelings from you
and make everything better
but I know that these feelings
will only help you to grow
and understand more about life
These feelings will help you
to become a more sensitive person
So as I watch your eyes
which tell me everything
I will offer you my
understanding and support
I will offer you my
love
I will offer you the
promise that your beautiful
smile will soon return

Monday, July 31

Tuesday, August 1

Wednesday, August 2

Thursday, August 3

Friday, August 4

Saturday, August 5

Sunday, August 6

Every day
I am astounded
to hear you talk
    so intelligently
Your wisdom grows
    and grows
as you do
You are such a delight
such a joy
such a beautiful person
The love I see
    in your eyes for me
is so moving and rewarding
And I hope you
    see and feel
the infinite love I have for you
Whatever you do
wherever you go
know that
I am here
in every way
for you

August 2017

Sunday	Monday	Tuesday	Wednesday
		1 **PAPA'S B-DAY**	2
6	7 Civic Holiday (Canada) Bank Holiday (Ireland/Scotland) Full Moon ○	8	9
13	14	15	16
20	21	22	23
27	28 Bank Holiday (UK except Scotland)	29	30

Notes:

Thursday	Friday	Saturday
3	4	5
10	11	12
17	18	19
24	25	26
		Women's Equality Day (USA)
31		

July							September						
S	M	T	W	T	F	S	S	M	T	W	T	F	S
						1						1	2
2	3	4	5	6	7	8	3	4	5	6	7	8	9
9	10	11	12	13	14	15	10	11	12	13	14	15	16
16	17	18	19	20	21	22	17	18	19	20	21	22	23
23/30	24/31	25	26	27	28	29	24	25	26	27	28	29	30

Notes:

Monday, August 7

Civic Holiday (Canada)
Bank Holiday (Ireland/Scotland)
Full Moon ○

Tuesday, August 8

Wednesday, August 9

.

Thursday, August 10

Friday, August 11

Saturday, August 12

Sunday, August 13

Monday, August 14

Tuesday, August 15

Wednesday, August 16

Thursday, August 17

Friday, August 18

Saturday, August 19

Sunday, August 20

You are such an outstanding person
and I hope nothing ever changes
your inner beauty
As you keep growing
remember always
to look at things the way you do now —
with sensitivity
honesty
compassion
and a touch of innocence...

(continued)

Monday, August 21

Tuesday, August 22

Wednesday, August 23

Thursday, August 24

Friday, August 25

Saturday, August 26   Women's Equality Day (USA)

Sunday, August 27

$\mathcal{R}$emember that people and situations
may not always be
as they appear
but if you remain true to yourself
it will be all right
With your outlook, you will see
the good in everything
and this will reflect back to you
When I look ahead
I see happiness for you on every level
and I am so glad
because that is what every mother
wishes for her daughter
I love you

Always have dreams.
Always try to make them a reality.

Monday, August 28　　　　　　　　　　　Bank Holiday (UK except Scotland)

Tuesday, August 29

Wednesday, August 30

Thursday, August 31

Friday, September 1　　　　　　　　　　　Eid al-Adha

Saturday, September 2

Sunday, September 3

Notes:

September 2017

Sunday	Monday	Tuesday	Wednesday

August

S	M	T	W	T	F	S
		1	2	3	4	5
6	7	8	9	10	11	12
13	14	15	16	17	18	19
20	21	22	23	24	25	26
27	28	29	30	31		

October

S	M	T	W	T	F	S
1	2	3	4	5	6	7
8	9	10	11	12	13	14
15	16	17	18	19	20	21
22	23	24	25	26	27	28
29	30	31				

Sunday	Monday	Tuesday	Wednesday
3	4 Labor Day (USA/Canada)	5	6 Full Moon ○
10 National Grandparents Day (USA)	11 Patriot Day (USA)	12	13
17	18	19	20
24	25	26	27

Notes:

Thursday	Friday	Saturday
	1	2
	Eid al-Adha	
7	8	9
14	15	16
21	22	23
UN International Day of Peace Rosh Hashanah Islamic New Year	Autumn Begins	
28	29	30
		Yom Kippur

Monday, September 4

Tuesday, September 5

Wednesday, September 6

Full Moon ○

Thursday, September 7

Friday, September 8

Saturday, September 9

Sunday, September 10

National Grandparents Day (USA)

I often marvel at your strength
to not give in to current misguided
morals and trends
I look at others your age —
some going through life aimlessly
and I know your journey
must be tough and lonely
because it is hard to be an individual
in a world of followers
where it is easy to go along with the crowd
It is so important for people
to actually choose the way to conduct their lives
And because you have done this
your relationships and accomplishments
will be genuinely deserved
and though there may not be a lot of people
with whom you will feel a kindred spirit
the people you find who are similar to yourself
will be the ones
who stand apart from the crowd
They, like you
will make a difference
in the world
with their dreams and actions

Monday, September 11

Patriot Day (USA)

Tuesday, September 12

Wednesday, September 13

Thursday, September 14

Friday, September 15

Saturday, September 16

Sunday, September 17

Be a part of as many things as possible
Soak up everything
Look everywhere
Feed your spirit
Feel different emotions
Be extremely curious
Think differently than what is expected
Touch nature
Search humanism
Now is NOT the time to limit possibilities
Now IS the time to experiment
Now IS the time to learn and grow
Now IS the time to explore
life's potential

Monday, September 18

Tuesday, September 19

Wednesday, September 20

Thursday, September 21

UN International Day of Peace
Rosh Hashanah
Islamic New Year

Friday, September 22

Autumn Begins

Saturday, September 23

Sunday, September 24

To see you happy —
laughing and dancing
smiling and content
striving toward goals of your own
accomplishing what you set out to do
having fun alone and with your friends
capable of loving and being loved
is what I have always wished for you...

(continued)

Monday, September 25

Tuesday, September 26

Wednesday, September 27

Thursday, September 28

Friday, September 29

Saturday, September 30   Yom Kippur

Sunday, October 1   National Breast Cancer Awareness Month Begins (USA)

Today I thought about your beautiful face
and felt your excitement for life
and your genuine happiness
and I am so proud of you as I realize that
my dreams for you have come true
What an extraordinary person you are
and as you continue to grow
please remember always
how very much
I love you

October 2017

Sunday	Monday	Tuesday	Wednesday
1 National Breast Cancer Awareness Month Begins (USA)	2	3	4
8	9 Columbus Day Observed (USA) Thanksgiving Day (Canada)	10	11
15	16	17	18
22	23	24	25
29 UK/Ireland Daylight Saving Time Ends	30 Bank Holiday (Ireland)	31 Halloween	

Thursday	Friday	Saturday
5 First Day of Succoth Full Moon ◯	6	7
12	13	14
19	20	21
26	27	28

September						
S	M	T	W	T	F	S
					1	2
3	4	5	6	7	8	9
10	11	12	13	14	15	16
17	18	19	20	21	22	23
24	25	26	27	28	29	30

November						
S	M	T	W	T	F	S
				1	2	3	4
5	6	7	8	9	10	11
12	13	14	15	16	17	18
19	20	21	22	23	24	25
26	27	28	29	30		

The freer you are with your emotions and feelings, the more you will be able to give and receive love.

Monday, October 2

Tuesday, October 3

Wednesday, October 4

Thursday, October 5

First Day of Succoth
Full Moon ○

Friday, October 6

Saturday, October 7

Sunday, October 8

Notes:

Monday, October 9

Tuesday, October 10

Wednesday, October 11

Thursday, October 12

Friday, October 13

Saturday, October 14

Sunday, October 15

Daughter, I Know That Your Dreams Will Come True

You are a unique person
and only you can do whatever
it takes to follow your dreams

So let your spirit lead you
on a path of excitement
and fulfillment
And know that
because you are a
determined and talented person
any dream that you dream
can become a reality

*A daughter is * a wonder *
a sweetness, a secret, an
artist * a perception, a delight*

Monday, October 16

Tuesday, October 17

Wednesday, October 18

Thursday, October 19

Friday, October 20

Saturday, October 21

Sunday, October 22

Notes:

Monday, October 23

Tuesday, October 24

Wednesday, October 25

Thursday, October 26

Friday, October 27

Saturday, October 28

Sunday, October 29   UK/Ireland Daylight Saving Time Ends

*I*f ever things are not
going well for you
and you have some problems to solve
If ever you are feeling confused
and don't know the right thing to do
If ever you are feeling frightened
and hurt
or if you just need someone
to talk to
please remember that
I am always here for you
ready to listen
without passing judgment
but with understanding
and love

Monday, October 30

Tuesday, October 31

Halloween

Wednesday, November 1

Thursday, November 2

Friday, November 3

Saturday, November 4

Full Moon ○

Sunday, November 5

Guy Fawkes Day (UK)
USA/Canada Daylight Saving Time Ends

Sometimes you
think that you
need to be perfect
that you cannot
make mistakes
At these times
you put so much
pressure on yourself
I wish that you
would realize
that you are
like everyone else —
capable of
reaching great potential
but not capable of
being perfect
So please
just do your best
and realize that
this is enough
Don't compare yourself
to anyone
Be happy to be
the wonderful
unique, very special
person that you are

November 2017

Sunday	Monday	Tuesday	Wednesday
			1
5 Guy Fawkes Day (UK) USA/Canada Daylight Saving Time Ends	**6**	**7** Election Day (USA)	**8**
12 Remembrance Sunday (UK)	**13**	**14**	**15**
19	**20**	**21**	**22**
26	**27**	**28**	**29**

October

S	M	T	W	T	F	S
1	2	3	4	5	6	7
8	9	10	11	12	13	14
15	16	17	18	19	20	21
22	23	24	25	26	27	28
29	30	31				

December

S	M	T	W	T	F	S
					1	2
3	4	5	6	7	8	9
10	11	12	13	14	15	16
17	18	19	20	21	22	23
24/31	25	26	27	28	29	30

Thursday	Friday	Saturday
2	3	4 Full Moon ○
9	10	11 Veterans Day (USA) Remembrance Day (Canada/Australia)
16	17	18
23 Thanksgiving Day (USA)	24	25
30 St. Andrew's Day (Scotland)		

Notes:

Monday, November 6

Tuesday, November 7   Election Day (USA)

Wednesday, November 8

Thursday, November 9

Friday, November 10

Saturday, November 11   Veterans Day (USA)
                                    Remembrance Day (Canada/Australia)

Sunday, November 12   Remembrance Sunday (UK)

If you know yourself well
and have developed a sense
of confidence in yourself
If you are honest with yourself
and honest with others
If you follow your heart
and adhere to your own truths
you are ready to share yourself
you are ready to set goals
you are ready to find happiness
And the more you love
and the more you give
and the more you feel
the more you will receive
from love
and the more you will receive
from life

Monday, November 13

Tuesday, November 14

Wednesday, November 15

Thursday, November 16

Friday, November 17

Saturday, November 18

Sunday, November 19

I want you to have a life of happiness
In order for you to have this
you must have many interests
and pursue them
You must have many goals
and work toward them
You must like your work
and always try to get better
You must consider yourself a success
by being proud of doing your best
You must have fun
You must listen to your own voice
You must have peace
and not always expect perfection
You must have respect
for yourself and others
My daughter, as I watch you grow up
I can see you are on the right path

Monday, November 20

Tuesday, November 21

Wednesday, November 22

Thursday, November 23   Thanksgiving Day (USA)

Friday, November 24

Saturday, November 25

Sunday, November 26

$\mathcal{M}$y daughter
I want to thank you
for being
the fine, sensitive, beautiful
person that you are
and extra thanks
for being
so easy to raise
You have made it
so easy for me
to be a parent
I will always love you

Monday, November 27

Tuesday, November 28

Wednesday, November 29

Thursday, November 30   St. Andrew's Day (Scotland)

Friday, December 1

Saturday, December 2

Sunday, December 3   Full Moon ○

$\mathcal{W}$hat makes people succeed
is the fact that they have confidence in themselves
and a very strong sense of purpose
They never have excuses for not doing something
and always try their hardest for perfection
They never consider the idea of failing
and they work extremely hard toward their goals
They know who they are
and they understand their weaknesses
as well as their strong points
They can accept and benefit from criticism
and they know when to defend what they are doing
They are creative people
who are not afraid to be a little different
You are one of these rare people
and it is so exciting to watch you
on your path to success
as you follow your dreams
and make them a reality

December 2017

Sunday	Monday	Tuesday	Wednesday

November

S	M	T	W	T	F	S
			1	2	3	4
5	6	7	8	9	10	11
12	13	14	15	16	17	18
19	20	21	22	23	24	25
26	27	28	29	30		

January 2018

S	M	T	W	T	F	S
	1	2	3	4	5	6
7	8	9	10	11	12	13
14	15	16	17	18	19	20
21	22	23	24	25	26	27
28	29	30	31			

Sunday	Monday	Tuesday	Wednesday
3 Full Moon ○	**4**	**5**	**6**
10	**11**	**12**	**13** First Day of Hanukkah
17	**18**	**19**	**20**
24 **31**	**25** Christmas	**26** First Day of Kwanzaa (USA) Boxing Day (Canada/UK/Australia) St. Stephen's Day (Ireland)	**27**

Thursday	Friday	Saturday
	1	2
7 National Pearl Harbor Remembrance Day (USA)	8	9
14	15	16
21 Winter Begins	22	23
28	29	30

Notes:

Notes:

Monday, December 4

Tuesday, December 5

Wednesday, December 6

Thursday, December 7   National Pearl Harbor Remembrance Day (USA)

Friday, December 8

Saturday, December 9

Sunday, December 10

Monday, December 11

Tuesday, December 12

Wednesday, December 13   First Day of Hanukkah

Thursday, December 14

Friday, December 15

Saturday, December 16

Sunday, December 17

Do what you love
Control your own life
Have imaginative, realistic dreams
Work hard
Make mistakes but learn from them
Believe in yourself but know your limitations
Ignore people who tell you that you can't
Plow through obstacles and failures
Try to turn your dreams into reality

Monday, December 18

Tuesday, December 19

Wednesday, December 20

Thursday, December 21

Winter Begins

Friday, December 22

Saturday, December 23

Sunday, December 24

You are so modest
that you really don't know or believe
how you are viewed by others
and in a way, that is nice
People respect and admire you
They see you as being extremely
intelligent and knowledgeable
strong and tenacious
creative and innovative
sensitive and kind
moral and honorable
fair and pretty
fun-loving and witty
athletic and vigorous
They see you as
a leader
a thinker
a doer
I think you possess all of
these attributes and more
and you don't even know it
which keeps you unassuming
and in a way, that is nice
Words cannot express
how proud I am of you
Only my heart can show you
how much I love you

Monday, December 25   Christmas

Tuesday, December 26

First Day of Kwanzaa (USA)
Boxing Day (Canada/UK/Australia)
St. Stephen's Day (Ireland)

Wednesday, December 27

Thursday, December 28

Friday, December 29

Saturday, December 30

Sunday, December 31